Inhalt

CD: Track 1–33

Lieder, Dialoge, Reime und Geschichten zu den Aufgaben

Bonustracks – Lieder

One man went to mow[1] ▪ CD: Track 34
Are you hungry?[1] ▪ CD: Track 35
Head and shoulders[2] ▪ CD: Track 36
Eight wild animals[1] ▪ CD: Track 37
The wheels on the bike[1] ▪ CD: Track 38

(Melodien: traditionell; [1]Text/Adaption: Renz/Schmutz; [2]Text: traditionell)

Lege die  auf die roten Lösungsfelder, dann werden die richtigen Ergebnisse sichtbar.

Auf einen Blick:

check:	kontrolliere
colour in:	male aus
complete:	ergänze
cross out:	streiche durch
draw:	zeichne
draw lines:	verbinde
fill in:	fülle aus
guess:	rate
listen:	hör zu
number:	nummeriere
point to:	zeige auf
read:	lies
speak:	sprich
tick:	hake ab
write:	schreibe

Aufgepasst:

Die Aufgaben mit einer  sind etwas schwieriger.

On the farm

CD: 2

1 Listen and number the animals.

CD: 3

2 Listen and speak.

3 Write the names of the animals.

CD: 4

4 Listen to the song and point to the picture.
Sing along.

One man went to mow,

went to mow a meadow.

One man and his pig,

went to mow a meadow.

CD: 5

5 Listen and read.
Then draw the animals.

This animal is pink.
It has got a funny little tail. 

This animal has got
four legs and warm fur. 

This animal has got
two legs and feathers. 

This animal has got horns.
It eats grass. It's not a cow. 

At home

CD: 6

1 Listen and point: Find the things.

CD: 7

2 Write the words. Speak the sentences and listen.

The  is in the children's __ __ __ __ __ __ __.

The 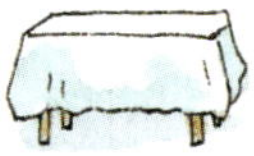 is in the __ __ __ __ __ __ __.

The  is in the parents' __ __ __ __ __ __ __.

The  is in the __ __ __ __ __ __   __ __ __ __.

The  is in the __ __ __ __ __ __ __ __.

Tipp Wenn du auf Englisch nach der Toilette fragen willst, sagst du: "Where's the toilet, please?"

CD: 8

3 Listen and point to the pictures.
Find the wrong picture. Cross it out.

1 

2 

3 

4 

4 My dream house: Write sentences.

My dream house has got ______________________

____

____

____

5 Draw a picture of your dream house.

My room

CD: 9

1 Listen and draw lines. Speak and point to the right picture.

The sofa is red.

The chair is pink.

The bed is green.

The cupboard is blue.

The lamp is yellow.

The desk is orange.

2 Can you find the words? Write them down.

c	u	p	b	o	a	r	d
k	s	d	e	v	o	n	y
s	o	f	d	l	a	m	p
r	f	o	f	a	m	g	j
r	a	a	d	e	s	k	t
f	t	c	h	a	i	r	l

Tipp Wenn du sagen willst, wo sich etwas befindet, helfen dir diese Wörter weiter:

under (unter)

next to (neben)

in (im/in)

on (auf)

CD: 10

3 What a mess! Can you answer William's questions? Listen and check.

4 Read and draw.

The cat is under the chair.
The cap is on the bed.
The car is next to the table.
The ball is in the cupboard.

Meals

CD: 11

1 Listen to the song and point to the pictures.

CD: 12

2 Listen and tick. What do you like?

[redacted]

	orange juice	lemonade	milk	hot chocolate	water	tea	coffee
William							
Lucy							

CD: 13

3 Complete the words. Listen and speak.

bread	toast
butter	ham
egg	honey
jam	roll
cornflakes	

1 ___ ___ ea ___

2 ___ u ___ ___ ___ ___

3 ___ o ___ ey

4 ___ oa ___ ___

5 j ___ ___

6 ___ a ___

7 corn ___ ___ ___ ___ ___ ___

8 ___ o ___ l

9 ___ gg

4 Find the words.

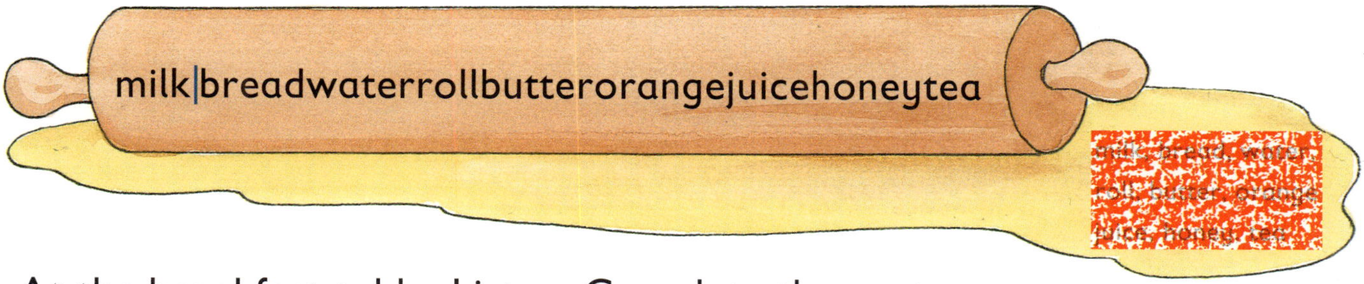

CD: 14

5 At the breakfast table: Listen. Complete the sentences.

Can you pass me the ___ and the ___, please?

Can I have the ___ and the ___, please?

Can you ___ me the ___ and the ___, please?

___ ___ ___ the ___ and ___, please?

In the restaurant

1 Read and draw lines.

CD: 15

2 A funny game: Listen and speak.
Then play the game.

⚀ fork  ⚁ knife  ⚂ cup 

⚃ spoon  ⚄ plate  ⚅ glass 

I eat my pizza with a ______________________ .

I eat my tomato soup with a ______________________ .

I drink my water in a ______________________ .

I eat my sausage with a ______________________ .

I eat my salad with a ______________________ .

I drink my hot chocolate in a ______________________ .

CD: 16

3 Listen. Then number.

Yes, please. I'd like a glass of orange juice.

Anything else?

Can I help you?

I'd like a carrot soup and sausages with salad, please.

Would you like anything to drink?

That's it. Thank you very much.

I'd like ___ ___ ___ ___ k ___ ___ .

Tipp "I'd like ..." ist die Kurzform von "I would like ..." und heißt: „Ich hätte gern ...".

4 Find the matching words. Colour them in.

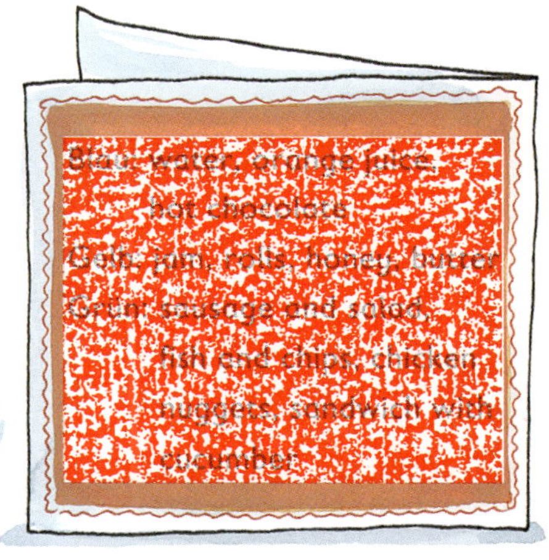

drinks | breakfast | lunch

sausage and salad | chicken nuggets | butter | water | rolls | honey | hot chocolate | jam | orange juice | sandwich with cucumber | fish and chips

5 Write your own menu.

Story: The three goats

CD: 17

1 Listen to the story.

This is family Flock. Father and Mother Flock and little Goaty Flock. They are all very hungry and dream of fresh, green grass.

The best green and juicy grass is on the other side of the river. No problem! There is a bridge over the river.

Under the bridge lives a grumpy and ugly giant. The giant is hungry, too, but he doesn't like grass and he doesn't like apples either …

First, little Goaty trots over the bridge.
"Who is trotting over MY bridge?", the ugly giant grumbles.
"It's just me", Goaty says nervously.

"Stop! I didn't have breakfast and you look so tasty! Yummy, yummy …"
"No, don't eat ME! The next goat is much bigger and tastier.", says Goaty.

Now, Mum and Dad trot over the bridge.
"Who is trotting over MY bridge?"
"It's NOT your tasty breakfast!", Mum and Dad say. They lower their horns.

The ugly giant gets very nervous and he shouts: "No problem. I'm not so hungry today. I better have a bath first!"
And he jumps into the river.

CD: 18

2 Read and tick. Listen and check.

	right	wrong
1. The goat family is not hungry.		
2. The goats eat sausages.		
3. The giant is hungry.		
4. Mum and Dad trot over the bridge.		
5. Mum and Dad lower their horns.		
6. Little Goaty jumps into the river.		

3 Do the crossword.

The goats are __ __ __ __ __ !
1 2 3 4 5

At the doctor's

CD: 19, 20

1 Listen and point. Then do the actions.

Head  and shoulders  ,
knees  and toes  , knees and toes.
Head and shoulders,
knees and toes, knees and toes.
And eyes  and ears 
and mouth  and nose  .
Head and shoulders,
knees and toes, knees and toes.

CD: 21

2 Fill in. Listen and check.

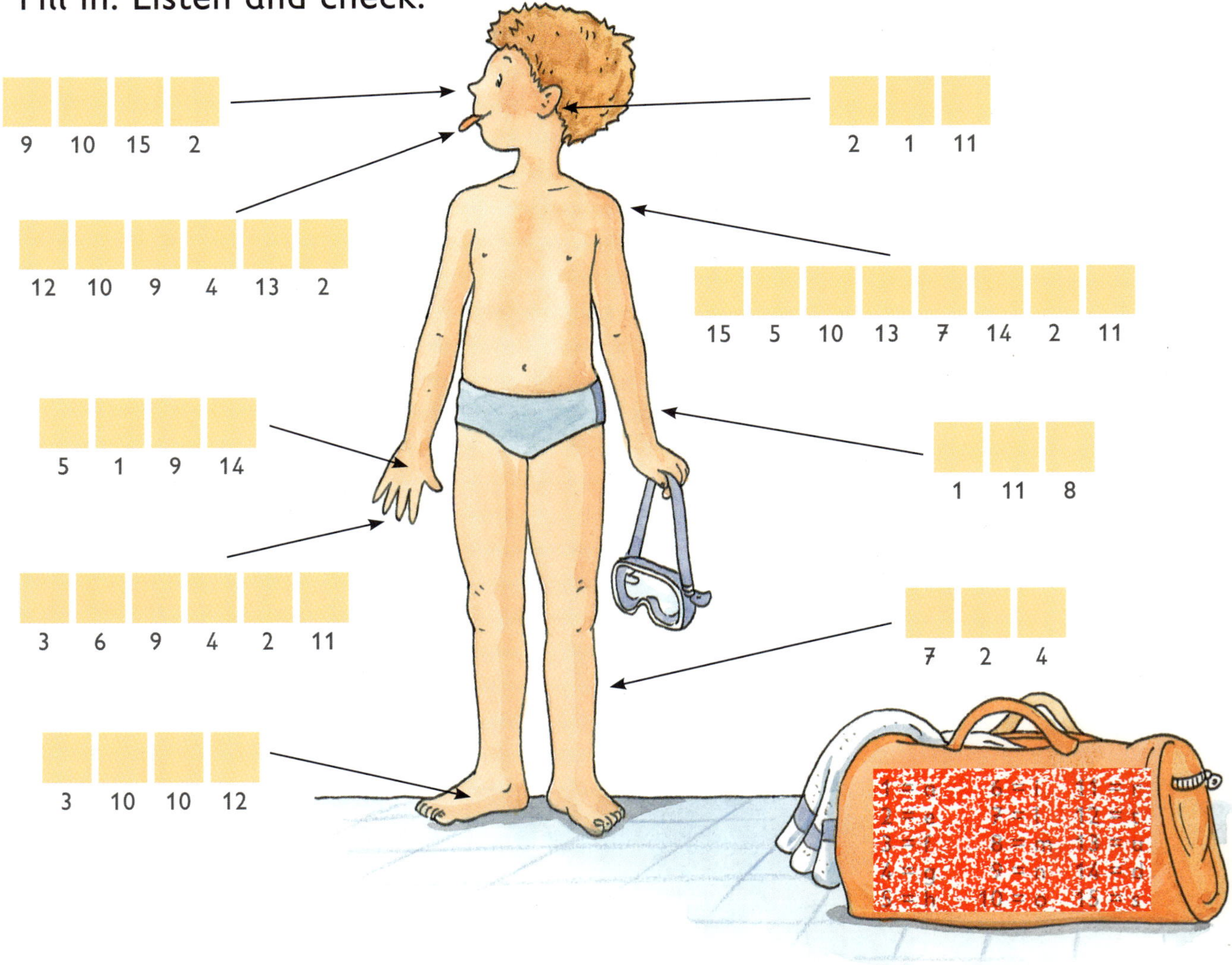

CD: 22

3 Listen to the dialogue. Then draw lines.

William sagt, dass sein Arm wehtut.

Die Mutter meint, dass sie zusammen zum Arzt gehen sollten.

Die Ärztin bittet William herein.

Die Ärztin fragt William, was ihm fehlt.

William sagt, dass er gestürzt ist und sein Arm wehtut.

Die Ärztin untersucht William und sagt, dass der Arm gebrochen ist.

CD: 23

4 What do the children and Konfetti tell the doctor? Fill in.

foot	*ear*	*tooth*
back	*head*	

Sally: My tooth ______ hurts.

Mike: My ______ hurts.

Amy: My ______ .

Tom: My ______ .

Konfetti: ______ .

CD: 24

1 a) Listen and draw lines.
b) Listen and speak.

1 

2 

3 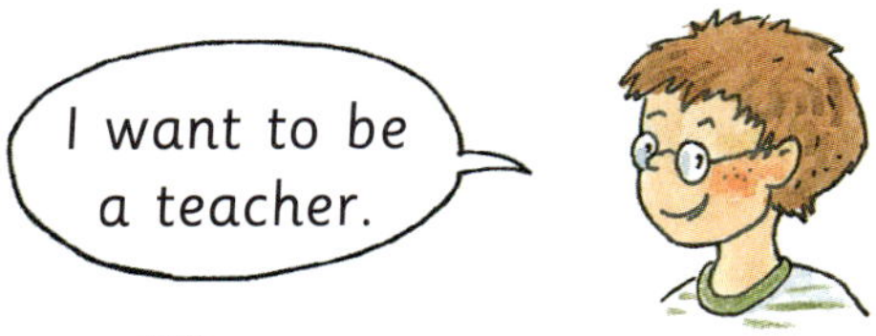

4 

5 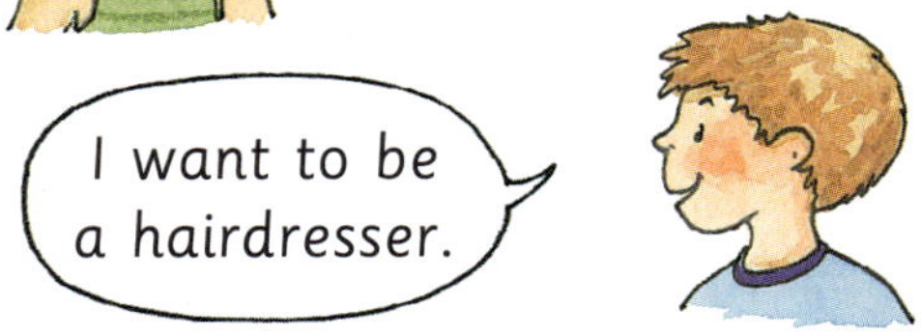

6 

a 

b 

c 

d 

e 

f 

Tipp Beachte: fire<u>man</u> bedeutet Feuerwehrmann und fire<u>woman</u> bedeutet Feuerwehrfrau.

2 What do you want to be?
Write and draw.

I want to be ______

a ______.

CD: 25

3 Fill in. Listen and control.

A ______________ puts out fires. 

A ______________ gives you medicine. 

A ______________ drives a truck. 

A ______________ teaches children. 

A ______________ cuts hair. 

A ______________ delivers letters. 

4 My jobs at home. Read and tick.

1. ☐ I make my bed. (S)
   ☐ I help in the garden. (T)

2. ☐ I go to the doctor's. (A)
   ☐ I feed my cat. (U)

3. ☐ I go to bed. (Z)
   ☐ I help in the kitchen. (P)

4. ☐ I do my homework. (E)
   ☐ I eat carrot soup. (U)

5. ☐ I feed the goat. (B)
   ☐ I lay the table. (R)

That was __ __ __ __ __!

Wild animals

CD: 26

1 Listen and point. Sing along.

Eight wild animals were living in the zoo.
And off there went the elephant,
the others wanted, too.

One wild animal was living in the zoo.
And off there went the long, long snake,
do you think that is true?

2 Find the words. Circle them.

A	B	Z	T	U	F	G	K	O	P	P	N	P	G
K	P	E	L	E	P	H	A	N	T	Y	L	O	I
T	M	B	T	P	K	I	S	R	M	T	I	P	R
R	O	R	L	K	S	P	R	T	Z	U	O	N	A
S	N	A	K	E	T	P	U	T	O	P	N	U	F
T	Z	M	A	T	M	O	N	K	E	Y	N	W	F
G	Z	U	T	F	U	S	I	R	T	A	L	M	E
C	R	O	C	O	D	I	L	E	H	K	I	P	O

elephant	giraffe
crocodile	lion
zebra	snake
hippo	monkey

CD: 27

3 Guess the animals. Listen and check.

This animal eats  leaves.
It can run. It has got long legs.
It's yellow and brown.
It's the ____________________.

This animal eats  meat.
It's  dangerous. It can run fast.
It's the king of the animals.
It's the ____________________.

This animal is big and fat.
It's grey. It eats grass.
It has got big ears and a  trunk.
It's the ____________________.

This animal is long and green.
It can swim. It has got many teeth.
It's  dangerous.
It's the ____________________.

4 What is your favourite wild animal?

My favourite wild animal is the ____________________
____
____
____________________.

Travelling and vehicles

CD: 28

1 Listen and look at the pictures. Sing along.

The wheels on the bike
go round and round,
round and round, round and round.
The wheels on the bike
go round and round.
All day long.

The people in the bus
stand up, sit down.

The conductor in the train
says: "Tickets please!"

The engine of the car
goes broom-broom-broom.

The pilot of the plane
says: "Welcome aboard!"

The captain on the ship
is looking out.

2 Find the vehicles and write them down.

carormbusbananatraincatplanelemonadeshipicebike

3 Follow the lines and write.

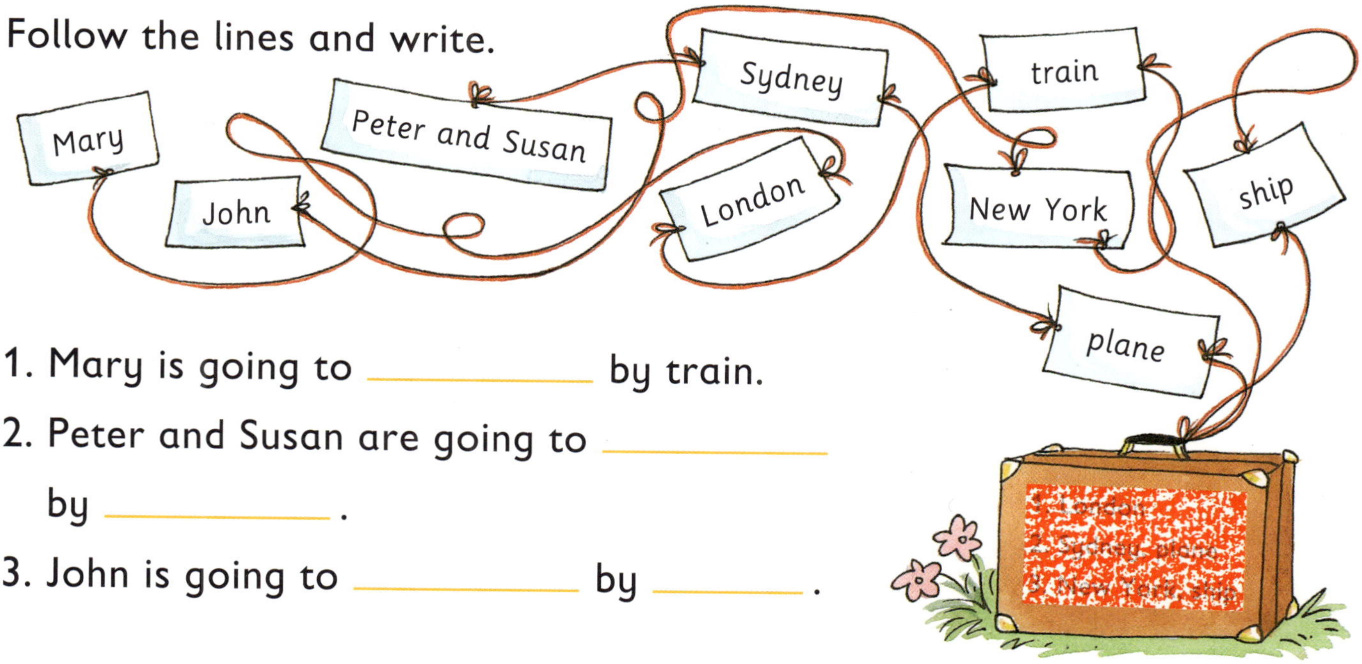

1. Mary is going to ____________ by train.
2. Peter and Susan are going to ____________ by ____________ .
3. John is going to ____________ by ____________ .

CD: 29

4 Listen and read. Colour in.

The traffic light
Red on top,
green below.
Red means stop,
green means go.
Yellow means wait,
even if you're late!

5 Look, read and tick.

right	wrong	
☐	☐	1. The traffic light is green.
☐	☐	2. The car has to wait.
☐	☐	3. The bus is yellow.
☐	☐	4. There are no people in the bus.
☐	☐	5. The traffic light is red.
☐	☐	6. Karlo is riding a bike.

On holiday

CD: 30

1 Listen.

CD: 31

2 Listen and speak. Fill in the words.

William is on the _ _ _ _ _.

He has got a _ _ _ _ _, sun cream and sunglasses with him.

In the sand there are _ _ _ _ _ _ _ _ _.

Far away you can see the _ _ _ _ _ _ _ _ _.

It's very hot. William is eating an _ _ _ cream.

CD: 32

3 Lucy is on the beach.
Read and draw.

The sun is shining.
Lucy is wearing sunglasses.
The towel is red.
Lucy is eating an ice cream.
There are three seashells in the sand.
Far away there are two mountains.

CD: 33

4 a) Listen and draw lines.

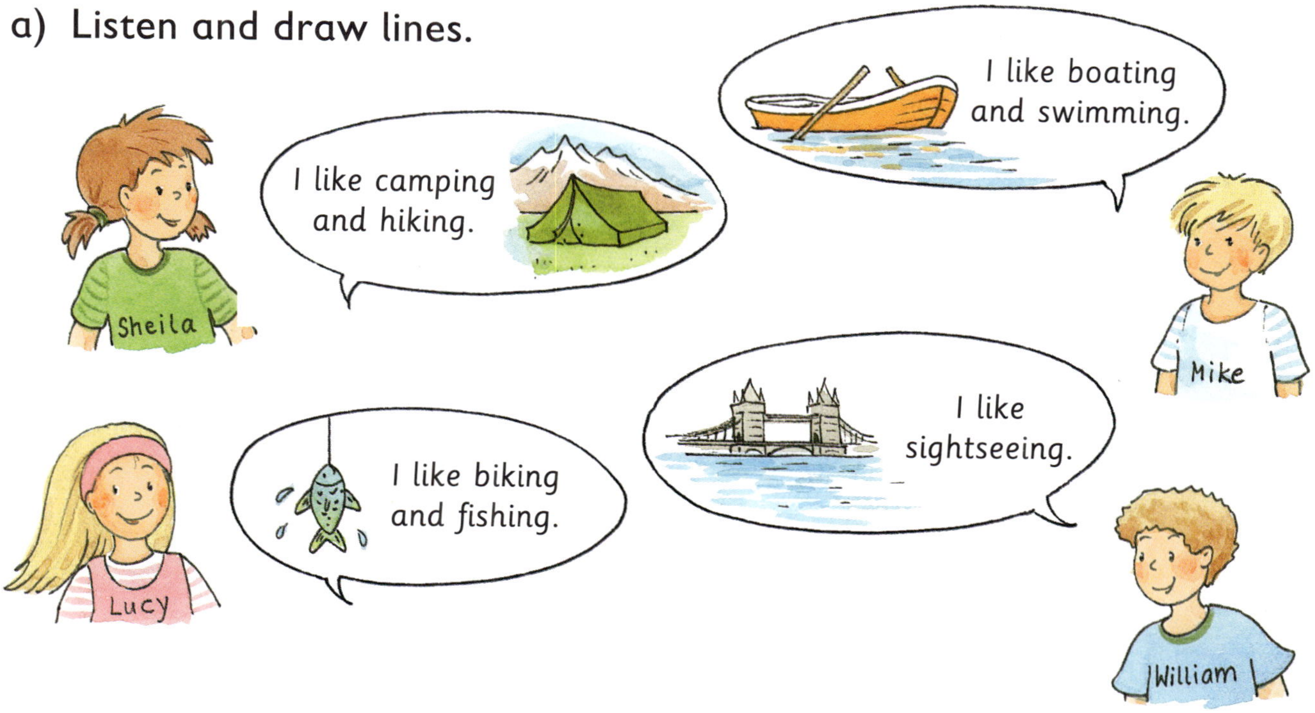

Tipp Wenn du von deinen Vorlieben sprechen möchtest, sagst du zum Beispiel: "I like swimm<u>ing</u>."

b) Is it Lucy, William, Sheila or Mike?
Fill in the names.

____________ wants to go to the beach.

____________ wants to go to the mountains.

____________ wants to go to the country.

____________ wants to go to the city.

5 Where do you want to go?
Write and draw.

I want to go to the ____________ .

I like ________________ .

Let's play: Get the flag!

RELAX!
Wo ist die Toilette?
RELAX!
Das Sofa ist rot.
Konfetti ist unter dem Bett.
RELAX!
Wo ist mein Teddy?

Dictionary

Manche Wörter sind im Englischen und Deutschen ähnlich oder sogar gleich. Sie unterscheiden sich nur in ihrer Aussprache.
Achte deshalb genau darauf, wie die Wörter auf der CD ausgesprochen werden.
Vielleicht können dir auch deine Eltern oder Geschwister die Wörter vorlesen.

A

action	Handlung
all	alle
animal	Tier
answer	Antwort; antworten
anything	(irgend)etwas
Anything else?	Noch etwas?
apple	Apfel
arm	Arm
at home	zu Hause

B

back	Rücken
ball	Ball
bath	Bad
bathroom	Badezimmer
be	sein
beach	Strand
bed	Bett
bedroom	Schlafzimmer
below	unten
best	beste/r/s
better	besser
big	groß
bike	Fahrrad
biking	Rad fahren
biscuit	Keks
blue	blau
boating	Boot fahren
book	Buch
bowl	Schüssel
bread	Brot
breakfast	Frühstück
bridge	Brücke
broken	gebrochen
brown	braun
bus	Omnibus
butter	Butter

C

camping	Zelten
can	können
cap	Mütze
captain	Kapitän
car	Auto
carrot	Karotte
cat	Katze
chair	Stuhl, Sessel
check	kontrollieren
cheese	Käse
chicken	Huhn
child, children	Kind, Kinder
chocolate	Schokolade
city	Stadt
climb	klettern
coffee	Kaffee
colour in	anmalen
complete	ergänzen
conductor	Schaffner
control	kontrollieren
cornflakes	Cornflakes
country	Land
cow	Kuh
crocodile	Krokodil
cross out	durchstreichen
crossword	Kreuzworträtsel
cucumber	Gurke
cup	Tasse
cupboard	Schrank
cut	schneiden

D

dangerous	gefährlich
day	Tag
deliver	zustellen, liefern
desk	Schreibtisch
dialogue	Gespräch
do	tun, machen
doctor	Arzt, Ärztin
dog	Hund
draw	zeichnen
draw lines	verbinden
dream	Traum; träumen
drink	Getränk; trinken
drive	fahren

E

ear	Ohr
eat	essen
egg	Ei
elephant	Elefant
engine	Motor
even if	selbst wenn
eye	Auge

F

family	Familie
fantastic	fantastisch
far away	weit weg, in der Ferne
farm	Bauernhof
fast	schnell
fat	dick, fett
father	Vater
favourite	Lieblings-
feather	Feder
feed	füttern
fell down	fiel hin
fill in	ausfüllen
find	finden
finger	Finger
fire	Feuer
fireman, firewoman	Feuerwehrmann, -frau
first	zuerst
fish and chips	Fisch mit Pommes
fishing	angeln
flag	Flagge
follow	folgen
foot, feet	Fuß, Füße
fork	Gabel
fresh	frisch
fridge	Kühlschrank
fruit	Obst, Frucht

funny	lustig
fur	Fell

G

game	Spiel
garden	Garten
get	werden
giant	Riese
giraffe	Giraffe
give	geben
glass	Glas
go	gehen
goat	Ziege
good	gut
grass	Gras
great	groß; großartig
green	grün
grey	grau
grumble	murren
grumpy	missmutig
guess	raten

H

hair	Haar, Haare
hairdresser	Friseur, Friseurin
ham	Schinken
hand	Hand
has got	hat
have	haben
head	Kopf
help	helfen
hen	Henne
hiking	wandern
hippo	Nilpferd
his	sein/e
holiday	Urlaub
homework	Hausaufgaben
honey	Honig; Liebling
horn	Horn
horse	Pferd
hot	heiß
house	Haus
hungry	hungrig
hurt	wehtun

I

I'd like …	Ich hätte gern …
I'm …	Ich bin …
ice cream	Eiskrem
ill	krank
in	im, in
into	hinein
it's/it is	es ist

J

jam	Marmelade
job	Arbeit, Aufgabe
juicy	saftig
jump	springen
just	nur

K

king	König
kitchen	Küche
knee	Knie
knife	Messer

L

lamp	Lampe
late	spät
lay the table	den Tisch decken
leaf, leaves	Blatt, Blätter
leg	Bein
lemonade	Limonade
Let's go!	Gehen wir!
letter	Brief
like	(gern) mögen
line	Linie
lion	Löwe
listen	(zu)hören
little	klein
live (in)	leben (in/im)
living room	Wohnzimmer
long	lang
look	(aus)sehen
looking out	Ausschau halten
lower	senken
lunch	Mittagessen
lunchtime	Mittagszeit

M

make	machen
man	Mann
many	viele
matching	passend
meadow	Wiese
meal	Mahlzeit
mean	bedeuten
meat	Fleisch
medicine	Medizin, Arznei
menu	Speisekarte
mess	Unordnung
milk	Milch
monkey	Affe
mother	Mutter
mountain	Berg
mouth	Mund
mow	(ab)mähen
much	viel
my	mein/e

N

name	Name
nervous	nervös
next to	neben
Next, please!	Der Nächste, bitte!
noodles	Nudeln
nose	Nase
number	Zahl; nummerieren
nurse	Kranken-schwester

O

off	fort, weg
old	alt
on	auf
on top	oben
one	eins; eine/r/s
orange	orange
orange juice	Orangensaft
other	andere/r/s
oven	Backofen
over	über

P

parents	Eltern
pass	geben, reichen
people	Menschen, Leute
picture	Bild
pig	Schwein
pilot	Pilot
pink	rosa

pizza	Pizza
plane	Flugzeug
plate	Teller
play	spielen
please	bitte
point (to)	zeigen (auf)
pony	Pony
postwoman	Briefträgerin
put out	löschen

Q

question	Frage

R

read	lesen
red	rot
relax	entspannen
restaurant	Restaurant
ride a bike	Rad fahren
right	richtig
river	Fluss
roll	Brötchen
room	Zimmer
round	rund
run	rennen, laufen

S

salad	Salat
sand	Sand
sandwich	belegtes Brötchen
sausage	Wurst
schoolbag	Schultasche
sea	Meer
seashell	Muschel
sentence	Satz
sheep	Schaf
shine	scheinen
ship	Schiff
shoe	Schuh
shoulder	Schulter
shout	schreien
side	Seite
sightseeing	Sehenswürdigkeiten besichtigen
Sing along!	Sing mit!
sit down	sich setzen
skateboarding	Skateboard fahren
smart	klug, schlau
snake	Schlange
sofa	Sofa
song	Lied
soup	Suppe
spaghetti	Spagetti
speak	sprechen
spoon	Löffel
stand up	aufstehen
story	Geschichte
striped	gestreift
summer	Sommer
sun	Sonne
sun cream	Sonnencreme
sunglasses	Sonnenbrille
supper	Abendessen
swim, swimming	schwimmen

T

table	Tisch
tail	Schwanz
tasty	schmackhaft
tea	Tee
teach	unterrichten
teacher	Lehrer, Lehrerin
teddy	Teddy
tell	erzählen
terrific	toll
Thank you very much.	Vielen Dank.
their	ihr/e
thing	Ding, Sache
think	denken
thousands of	Tausende
tick	abhaken
ticket	Fahrkarte
time	Zeit
toast	Toast
today	heute
toe	Zehe
toilet	Toilette
tomato	Tomate
tongue	Zunge
too	auch
tooth, teeth	Zahn, Zähne
toothbrush	Zahnbürste
towel	Handtuch
toy	Spielzeug
traffic light	Ampel
train	Zug
travelling	reisen
trot	trotten
truck	Lastwagen
truck driver	Lastwagenfahrer
true	wahr
trunk	Rüssel

U

ugly	hässlich
under	unter

V

vehicle	Fahrzeug
very	sehr

W

wait	warten
want	wollen
warm	warm
water	Wasser
wear	tragen, anhaben
Welcome aboard!	Willkommen an Bord!
Well done!	Gut gemacht!
went	ging
What's the matter?	Was ist los?
wheel	Rad, Reifen
Where's ...?	Wo ist ...?
wild	wild
with	mit
word	Wort
write	schreiben
wrong	falsch

Y

yellow	gelb
your	dein/e
yummy	lecker

Z

zebra	Zebra
zoo	Zoo

Spiele zur Wörterliste

Mit diesen Spielen kannst du die Wörter der Wörterliste auf den Seiten 26 bis 28 regelmäßig üben. Viel Spaß!

Hangman (2 oder mehr Spieler)

Wähle ein Wort aus der Wörterliste, das die anderen erraten sollen. Für jeden Buchstaben zeichnest du einen Strich. Deine Mitspieler raten nun Buchstaben (möglichst auf Englisch): Kommt er vor, trägst du ihn an der richtigen Stelle ein, kommt er nicht vor, fängst du an, einen „hangman“ – ein Galgenmännchen – zu malen. Wird der „hangman“ fertig, hast du gewonnen. Errät ein Mitspieler das Wort, ist er der Sieger.

Wörterschlange (1 oder mehr Spieler)

Suche ein englisches Wort aus, das sich alle Mitspieler aufschreiben. Nun versucht jeder, die längste Wörterschlange zu bilden. Das nächste Wort muss dabei immer mit dem letzten Buchstaben beginnen: So folgt z. B. auf das Wort ca**t** ein Wort mit **t** wie **t**ea oder **t**able usw.

Wörtersuche (2 oder mehr Spieler)

Überlegt euch ein Merkmal, nach dem ihr Wörter suchen wollt, z. B. Wörter, die mit s beginnen, Wörter mit zwei Silben oder Tierbegriffe usw. Nun habt ihr drei Minuten Zeit. Gewinner ist, wer die meisten Wörter zu dem Merkmal gefunden hat.

Knack den Code

Code knacken und mit jedem Heft 14 Tage kostenlos online lernen auf scoyo.de*

Auf jeder Doppelseite findest du eine kleine braune Lupe. Darin steht jeweils eine Zahl.

- Schreibe die Zahlen nacheinander auf die Linien.
- Ersetze sie dann durch die Buchstaben, die auf dem Zettel versteckt sind: zum Beispiel 7 durch den Buchstaben U.
- Trage jeweils den passenden Buchstaben unter der Zahl ein. Wie heißt der Lösungssatz?

CODE

1 =	4 =
8 =	5 =
7 =	14 =
11 =	3 =
2 =	13 =
9 =	6 =
12 =	10 =
15 =	16 =

___ 7   ___ ___ 6 ___   ___ ___ 2

___ ___ 13 ___ ___ ___ 9 ___ ___ ___ 15 16 5 !

Hast du den Lösungssatz ermittelt? Dann kannst du online spielend weiterlernen auf scoyo.de. Notiere hier der Reihe nach die Buchstaben aus den grün markierten Feldern im Lösungssatz.

Besuche im Internet die Seite www.scoyo.de/ravensburger und gib dort die Buchstabenkombination aus dem Heft ein. Über 4000 Lerngeschichten und mehr als 10 000 Übungen und Tests warten auf dich.

Viel Spaß beim Lernen mit scoyo wünschen dir deine Lern-Detektive

* Keine Vertragsbindung, keine Verlängerung – Kinder können scoyo 14 Tage lang völlig unverbindlich und kostenfrei testen. Die Testphase endet automatisch und ist mit keinerlei Verpflichtungen verbunden. Eine Kündigung ist nicht erforderlich.

Ausschneidebogen

Spielanleitung: Get the flag!

Du brauchst:
1 Mitspieler, 2 Spielfiguren,
1 Würfel

Vorbereitung:
Schneidet die Flaggen aus und legt sie auf einen Stapel. Einigt euch, wer das linke und wer das rechte Flaggenfeld auf dem Spielplan bekommt. Stellt beide Spielfiguren an den Start.
Ziel des Spiels ist es, möglichst schnell 10 Flaggen zu sammeln.

Der erste Spieler würfelt und zieht die gewürfelte Augenzahl auf den Feldern.
Die Spielfelder bedeuten:
Würfel: Würfle noch einmal!
Relax: Setze einmal aus!
Bild: Nenne das englische Wort!
Sprechblase: Übersetze den Satz!
Für jede richtige Antwort erhaltet ihr eine Flagge. Legt sie auf ein freies Flaggenfeld.

Gewinner ist, wer als Erster alle Flaggenfelder auf seiner Seite belegt hat.

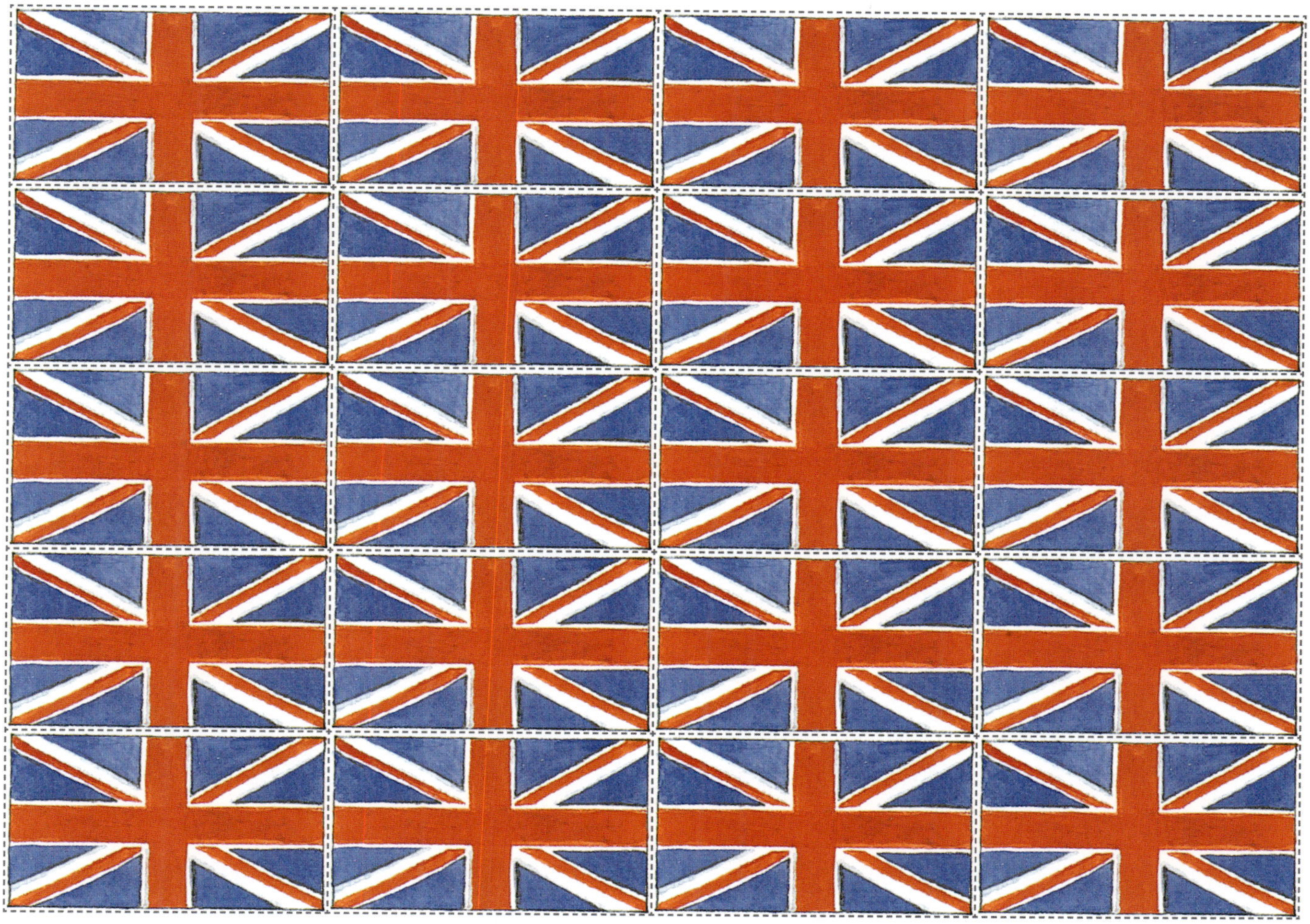

Very good!	Well done!	Super!	Wow!
Terrific!	Fantastic!	Great!	Nice work!
Good job!	Super!	Terrific!	Wow!
Fantastic!	Nice work!	Good job!	Great!
Well done!	Very good!	Wow!	Well done!